ÍNDICE

WRITER 5
    FUNCTION KEYS 6
    DIRECTION KEYS 7
    OTHER KEYS 7
    CAPITAL KEYS 8
    CONTROL KEYS 10
    CONTROL KEYS + FUNCTION KEYS 14
    CONTROL KEYS + ARROW KEYS 15
    CONTROL KEYS + OTHER KEYS 16
    CONTROL KEYS + CAPITAL KEYS 17
    CONTROL KEYS + ALT KEY 21
    ALT KEY 21
CALC 23
    FUNCTION KEYS 24
    DIRECTION KEYS 25
    OTHER KEYS 25
    CAPITAL KEYS 26
    CONTROL KEYS 28
    CONTROL KEYS + FUNCTION KEYS 32
    CONTROL KEYS + ARROW KEY 32
    CONTROL KEYS + OTHER KEYS 33
    CONTROL KEYS + CAPITAL KEYS 34
    CONTROL KEYS + CAPITAL + FUNCTION 37
    CONTROL KEYS + CAPITAL + ARROW KEY 37

- CONTROL KEYS + CAPITAL + OTHER KEYS 38
- CONTROL KEYS + ALT KEY 38
- ALT KEY 39

IMPRESS 41
- FUNCTION KEYS 42
- OTHER KEYS 43
- CAPITAL KEYS 43
- CONTROL KEYS 44
- CONTROL KEYS + FUNCTION KEYS 47
- CONTROL KEYS + OTHER KEYS 47
- CONTROL KEYS + CAPITAL KEYS 48
- CONTROL KEYS + ALT KEY 50
- ALT KEY 52

DRAW 55
- FUNCTION KEYS 56
- OTHER KEYS 57
- CAPITAL KEYS 57
- CONTROL KEYS 58
- CONTROL KEYS + FUNCTION KEYS 61
- CONTROL KEYS + OTHER KEYS 61
- CONTROL KEYS + CAPITAL KEYS 62
- CONTROL KEYS + ALT KEY 64
- ALT KEY 65

MATH 67
- FUNCTION KEYS 68
- OTHER KEYS 68
- CAPITAL KEYS + FUNCTION 69

- CONTROL KEYS 69
- CONTROL KEYS + FUNCTION KEYS 70
- CONTROL KEYS + OTHER KEYS 71
- CONTROL KEYS + CAPITAL KEYS 71
- ALT KEY 71

BASE 73
- FUNCTION KEYS 74
- OTHER KEYS 75
- CAPITAL KEYS 75
- CONTROL KEYS 76
- CONTROL KEYS + FUNCTION KEYS 79
- CONTROL KEYS + OTHER KEYS 80
- CONTROL KEYS + CAPITAL KEY 80
- CONTROL KEYS + CAPITAL + FUNCTION 82
- ALT KEY 82
- CONTROL KEYS + ALT 83

WRITER

FUNCTION KEYS

F1

Help.

F2

Formula.

F3

Execute text entry.

F4

Position and size (Chart option).

F5

Browser.

F6

Scroll through the program bar.

F7

Spelling.

F8

Extended selection enabled.

F9

Update fields.

F10

Activate the menu bar.

F11

Styles.

F12

Numbering.

DIRECTION KEYS

BELOW

Go to the Below

UP

Go to the up.

LEFT

Shift one character to the left.

RIGHT

Shift one character to the right.

OTHER KEYS

HOME

Go to the beginning of the line.

END
Go to the end of the line.

RE PÁG
Previous page.

AV PÁG
Next page.

INTRO
Insert paragraph.

SUPR
Delete content.

ESC
Cancel.

INSERT
Insertion mode.

CAPITAL KEYS

CAPITAL + F3
Change capitalization.

CAPITAL + F4
Go to next frame.

CAPITAL + F5

Restore edit view.

CAPITAL + F7

Automatic spell check.

CAPITAL + F8

Activate multiple selection.

CAPITAL + F9

Calculate table.

CAPITAL + F10

Display the context menu.

CAPITAL + F11

New.

CAPITAL + F12

Viñetas.

CAPITAL + BELOW

Selection down.

CAPITAL + UP

Selection up to the first line.

CAPITAL + LEFT

Select character on the left.

CAPITAL + RIGHT

Select character on the right.

CAPITAL + HOME

Select to the beginning of the line.

CAPITAL + END

Select to the end of the line.

CAPITAL + INSERT

Paste.

CAPITAL + SUPR

Cut.

CAPITAL + RE PÁG

Select to previous page.

CAPITAL + AV PÁG

Select to next page.

CAPITAL + INTRO

Insert manual line break.

CONTROL KEYS

CTRL + 0

Body text.

CTRL +1

Title 1.

CTRL + 2

Title 2.

CTRL + 3

Title 3.

CTRL + 4

Title 4.

CTRL + 5

Title 5.

CTRL + A

Open...

CTRL + B

Search.

CTRL + C

Copy.

CTRL + D

Double underline.

CTRL + E

Select all.

CTRL + F

Search.

CTRL + G

Save.

CTRL + H

Search and replace.

CTRL + I

Cursive.

CTRL + J

Justified alignment.

CTRL + K

Cursive.

CTRL + L

Alignment to the left.

CTRL + M

Clear format.

CTRL + N

Black.

CTRL + O

Open.

CTRL + P

Print.

CTRL + Q

Exit.

CTRL + R

Alignment to the right.

CTRL + S

Underlined.

CTRL + T

Centered alignment.

CTRL + U

New.

CTRL + V

Paste.

CTRL + W

Close window .

CTRL + X

Cut.

CTRL + Y

Redo.

CTRL + Z

Undo.

CTRL + [

Decrease.

CTRL +]

Increase.

CONTROL KEYS + FUNCTION KEYS

CTRL + F2

More fields...

CTRL + F3

Automatic text.

CTRL + F4

Close.

CTRL + F5

Sidebar.

CTRL + F7

Synonyms.

CTRL + F8

Mark fields.

CTRL + F9

Field names.

CTRL + F10

Formatting marks.

CTRL + F11

Set the focus on the combo box.

CTRL + F12

Table.

CONTROL KEYS + ARROW KEYS

CTRL + BELOW

Go to next paragraph.

CTRL + UP

Go to previous paragraph.

CTRL + LEFT

Ir a la Left de la palabra.

CTRL + RIGHT

Go to the right of the word.

CONTROL KEYS + OTHER KEYS

CTRL + HOME

Go to the beginning of the document.

CTRL + END

Go to the end of the document.

CTRL + REV PÁG

Go to header.

CTRL + AV PÁG

Go to the bottom of the page.

CTRL + INTRO

Page break.

CTRL + BACKSPACE KEY

Delete up to the beginning of the word.

CTRL + INSERT

Copy.

CTRL + SUPR

Delete until the end of the word.

CTRL + +

Calculate.

CTRL + -

Insert discretionary hyphen.

CTRL + *

Execute macro field.

CTRL + /

Optional invisible separation.

CONTROL KEYS + CAPITAL KEYS

CTRL + CAPITAL + 0

Default paragraph.

CTRL + CAPITAL + A

Left to right.

CTRL + CAPITAL + B

Subindex.

CTRL + CAPITAL + C

Record change tracking.

CTRL + CAPITAL + D

Right to left.

CTRL + CAPITAL + F

Repeat search.

CTRL + CAPITAL + I

Select text.

CTRL + CAPITAL + J

Full screen.

CTRL + CAPITAL + M

Editing mode.

CTRL + CAPITAL + N

Templates.

CTRL + CAPITAL + O

Print preview.

CTRL + CAPITAL + P

Superscript.

CTRL + CAPITAL + Q

Stop macro execution.

CTRL + CAPITAL + R

Rules.

CTRL + CAPITAL + S

Save as...

CTRL + CAPITAL + T

Do not protect Tables.

CTRL + CAPITAL + V

Special gluing.

CTRL + CAPITAL + X

Remove direct character formats.

CTRL + CAPITAL + Y

Repeat.

CTRL + CAPITAL + Z

Redo.

CTRL + CAPITAL + F4

Data origins.

CTRL + CAPITAL + F5

Go to page.

CTRL + CAPITAL + F8

Block area.

CTRL + CAPITAL + F9

Update fields for entries.

CTRL + CAPITAL + F11

Update.

CTRL + CAPITAL + F12

Deactivate numbering.

CTRL + CAPITAL + BELOW

Select to the end of the paragraph.

CTRL + CAPITAL + UP

Select up to the beginning of the paragraph.

CTRL + CAPITAL + LEFT

Select up to the beginning of the word.

CTRL + CAPITAL + RIGHT

Select to the end of the word.

CTRL + CAPITAL + HOME

Select to the beginning of the document.

CTRL + CAPITAL + END

Select to the end of the document.

CTRL + CAPITAL + AV PÁG

Edit footnote / endnote.

CTRL + CAPITAL + INTRO

Insert column break.

CTRL + CAPITAL + ESPACIO

Insert indivisible space.

CTRL + CAPITAL + BACKSPACE KEY

Delete up to the beginning of the sentence.

CONTROL KEYS + ALT KEY

CTRL + ALT + B

Search and replace.

CTRL + ALT + C

Coment.

CTRL + ALT + E

Extension manager.

CTRL + ALT + K

Hyperlink...

CTRL + ALT + BELOW

Move down one level in the list.

CTRL + ALT + UP

Move up one level in the list.

CTRL + ALT +CAPITAL + V

Paste plain text.

ALT KEY

ALT

Activate the menu bar.

ALT + X

Toggle Unicode notation.

ALT + BACKSPACE KEY

Undo.

ALT + CAPITAL + F8

Block area.

ALT + CAPITAL + ESPACIO

Insert indivisible narrow space.

ALT + F11

Basic.

ALT + F12

Options.

CALC

FUNCTION KEYS

F1

Help.

F2

Edit cell mode.

F4

Switch between cell reference types.

F5

Browser.

F7

Spelling.

F8

Extended selection status.

F9

Recalculate.

F10

Activate the menu bar.

F11

Styles.

F12

Group.

DIRECTION KEYS

BELOW

Download.

UP

Up.

LEFT

Move to the left.

RIGHT

Move to the right.

OTHER KEYS

HOME

Go to the beginning of the document.

END

Go to the end of the document.

REV PÁG

Go one page up.

AV PÁG

Go down one page.

ESC

Cancel.

BACKSPACE KEY

Empty cells...

SUPR

Delete content / Empty cells...

CAPITAL KEYS

CAPITAL + F3

Change capitalization.

CAPITAL + F5

Track dependencies.

CAPITAL + F7

Automatic spell check.

CAPITAL + F8

Complementary selection status.

CAPITAL + F9

Track precedents.

CAPITAL + F10

Display the context menu.

CAPITAL + F11

Save as template.

CAPITAL + BELOW

Select to the bottom line.

CAPITAL + UP

Select up to the top line.

CAPITAL + LEFT

Select to the left.

CAPITAL + RIGHT

Select to the right.

CAPITAL + INCIO

Select to the beginning of the document.

CAPITAL + END

Select to the end of the document.

CAPITAL + INSERT

Paste.

CAPITAL + SUPR

Cut.

CAPITAL + REV PÁG

Select page up.

CAPITAL + AV PÁG

Select page down.

CAPITAL + ESPACIO

Select row.

CAPITAL + BACKSPACE KEY

Undo selection.

CONTROL KEYS

CTRL + 1

Cell formatting.

CTRL + 2

Line spacing 2

CTRL + 5

Line spacing 1,5

CTRL + A

Open.

CTRL + B

Search.

CTRL + C

Copy.

CTRL + D

Fill down.

CTRL + E

Select all.

CTRL + F

Search.

CTRL + G

Save.

CTRL + H

Search and replace.

CTRL + I

Cursive.

CTRL + J

Justified alignment.

CTRL + K

Cursive.

CTRL + L

Align left.

CTRL + M

Clear format.

CTRL + N

Black.

CTRL + O

Open...

CTRL + P

Print.

CTRL + Q

Exit.

CTRL + R

Align right.

CTRL + S

Underlined.

CTRL + T

Center align.

CTRL + U

New.

CTRL + W

Close window

CTRL + X

Cut.

CTRL + Y

Redo.

CTRL + Z

Undo.

CTRL + ;

Insert current date.

CTRL + '

Copy top formula.

CTRL + [

Marcar los precedentes.

CTRL +]

Marcar los dependientes.

CTRL + ,

Insert current date.

CTRL + TABULACIÓN

Go to next page.

CONTROL KEYS + FUNCTION KEYS

CTRL + F2

Function...

CTRL + F3

Manage names.

CTRL + F4

Close.

CTRL + F5

Sidebar.

CTRL + F7

Synonyms.

CTRL + F8

Highlighting values.

CTRL + F12

DesGroup.

CONTROL KEYS + ARROW KEY

CTRL + BELOW

Go to bottom margin.

CTRL + UP

Go to top margin.

CTRL + LEFT

Go to left margin.

CTRL + RIGHT

Go to right margin.

CONTROL KEYS + OTHER KEYS

CTRL + HOME

Go to the beginning of the file.

CTRL + END

Go to the end of the file.

CTRL + REV PÁG

Go to previous page.

CTRL + INSERT

Copy.

CTRL + ESPACIO

Select columns.

CTRL + BACKSPACE KEY

Go to the current cell.

CTRL + +

Insert cells.

CTRL + -

Eliminar celdas.

CTRL + *

Mark data area.

CTRL + /

Select matrix formula.

CONTROL KEYS + CAPITAL KEYS

CTRL + CAPITAL + 1

Format cell number.

CTRL + CAPITAL + 2

Scientific cell format.

CTRL + CAPITAL + 3

Cell format date.

CTRL + CAPITAL + 4

Currency cell format.

CTRL + CAPITAL + 5

Cell format percentage.

CTRL + CAPITAL + 6

General cell formatting.

CTRL + CAPITAL + B

Subindex.

CTRL + CAPITAL + C

Record change tracking.

CTRL + CAPITAL + F

Repeat search.

CTRL + CAPITAL + J

Full screen.

CTRL + CAPITAL + M

Editing mode

CTRL + CAPITAL + N

Templates.

CTRL + CAPITAL + O

Print preview.

CTRL + CAPITAL + P

Superscript.

CTRL + CAPITAL + Q

Stop macro execution.

CTRL + CAPITAL + R

Redraw.

CTRL + CAPITAL + S

Save as...

CTRL + CAPITAL + T

Input field Table area.

CTRL + CAPITAL + V

Special gluing.

CTRL + CAPITAL + Y

Repeat.

CTRL + CAPITAL + Z

Redo.

CTRL + CAPITAL + ;

Insert current time.

CTRL + CAPITAL + ,

Insert current time.

CTRL + CAPITAL + TABULACIÓN

Go to previous page.

CONTROL KEYS + CAPITAL + FUNCTION

CTRL + CAPITAL + F2

Input line.

CTRL + CAPITAL + F4

Data origins.

CTRL + CAPITAL + F5

Table entry field.

CTRL + CAPITAL + F9

Unconditional recalculation.

CONTROL KEYS + CAPITAL + ARROW KEY

CTRL + CAPITAL + BELOW

Select to the bottom margin.

CTRL + CAPITAL + UP

Select to the top margin.

CTRL + CAPITAL + LEFT

Select to the left margin.

CTRL + CAPITAL + RIGHT

Select to the right margin.

CONTROL KEYS + CAPITAL + OTHER KEYS

CTRL + CAPITAL + HOME

Select to the beginning of the file.

CTRL + CAPITAL + END

Select to the end of the file.

CTRL + CAPITAL + REV PÁG

Select to previous page.

CTRL + CAPITAL + AV PÁG

Select to next page.

CTRL + CAPITAL + ESPACIO

Select all.

CONTROL KEYS + ALT KEY

CTRL + ALT + B

Search and replace.

CTRL + ALT + C

Coments.

CTRL + ALT + E

Extension manager.

CTRL + ALT + K

Hyperlink.

CTRL + ALT + CAPITAL + V

Paste plain text.

ALT KEY

ALT + BELOW

Selection list.

ALT + BACKSPACE KEY

Undo.

ALT

Activate the menu bar.

ALT + X

Switch Unicode notation.

ALT + F11

Basic.

ALT + F

Options...

IMPRESS

FUNCTION KEYS

F1
Help.

F2
Text box.

F3
Group login.

F5
Start presentation.

F6
Scrolling through the program bars.

F7
Spelling.

F8
Edit points.

F10
Activate the menu bar.

F11
Styles.

OTHER KEYS

RE PÁG

Go to previous page.

AV PÁG

Go to next page.

INTRO

Insert paragraph.

SUPR

Delete content.

CAPITAL KEYS

CAPITAL + F3

Duplicate.

CAPITAL + F4

Go to next frame.

CAPITAL + F5

Start from current slide.

CAPITAL + F10

Display the context menu.

CAPITAL + INSERT

Paste.

CAPITAL + SUPR

Cut.

CONTROL KEYS

CTRL +1

Line spacing 1.

CTRL + 2

Line spacing 2.

CTRL + 5

Line spacing 1,5.

CTRL + A

Open...

CTRL + B

Search.

CTRL + C

Copy.

CTRL + E

Select all.

CTRL + F

Search.

CTRL + G

Save.

CTRL + H

Search and replace.

CTRL + I

Cursive.

CTRL + J

Justified alignment.

CTRL + K

Cursive.

CTRL + L

Alignment to the left.

CTRL + M

New page.

CTRL + N

Black.

CTRL + O

Open.

CTRL + P

Print.

CTRL + Q

Exit.

CTRL + R

Alignment to the right.

CTRL + S

Underlined.

CTRL + T

Centered alignment.

CTRL + U

New.

CTRL + V

Paste.

CTRL + W

Close window .

CTRL + X

Cut.

CTRL + Y

Redo.

CTRL + Z

Undo.

CTRL + [

Decrease.

CTRL +]

Increase.

CONTROL KEYS + FUNCTION KEYS

CTRL + F3

Leave group.

CTRL + F4

Close.

CTRL + F5

Sidebar.

CTRL + F7

Synonyms.

CONTROL KEYS + OTHER KEYS

CTRL + INSERT

Copy.

CTRL + SUPR

Delete until the end of the word.

CTRL + +

Bring forward.

CTRL + -

Send back.

CTRL + *

Execute macro field.

CTRL + /

Optional invisible separation.

CONTROL KEYS + CAPITAL KEYS

CTRL + CAPITAL + B

Subindex.

CTRL + CAPITAL + G

Group.

CTRL + CAPITAL + K

Combine.

CTRL + CAPITAL + M

Clear format.

CTRL + CAPITAL + N

Templates

CTRL + CAPITAL + O

Print preview.

CTRL + CAPITAL + P

Superscript.

CTRL + CAPITAL + Q

Stop macro execution.

CTRL + CAPITAL + R

Rules.

CTRL + CAPITAL + S

Save as...

CTRL + CAPITAL + V

Special gluing.

CTRL + CAPITAL + Y

Repeat.

CTRL + CAPITAL + Z

Redo.

CTRL + CAPITAL + F4

Data origins.

CTRL + CAPITAL + F5

Browser.

CTRL + CAPITAL + F8

Fit to frame.

CTRL + CAPITAL + BELOW

Download the page.

CTRL + CAPITAL + UP

Upload page.

CTRL + CAPITAL + HOME

Move page to top.

CTRL + CAPITAL + END

Move page to end.

CTRL + CAPITAL + ESPACIO

Insert indivisible space.

CONTROL KEYS + ALT KEY

CTRL + ALT + B

Search and replace.

CTRL + ALT + C

Coment.

CTRL + ALT + E

Extension manager.

CTRL + ALT + K

Hyperlink...

CTRL + ALT + REV PÁG

Previous comment.

CTRL + ALT + AV PÁG

Next comment.

CTRL + ALT +CAPITAL + 9

Activate / Desactivate ItemBrowser.

CTRL + ALT +CAPITAL + G

DesGroup.

CTRL + ALT +CAPITAL + K

Split.

CTRL + ALT +CAPITAL + P

Pixel mode.

CTRL + ALT +CAPITAL + V

Paste plain text.

ALT KEY

ALT

Activate the menu bar.

ALT + BACKSPACE KEY

Undo.

ALT + CAPITAL + F5

Go to the last edited slide.

ALT + CAPITAL + F8

Block area.

ALT + CAPITAL + BELOW

Download.

ALT + CAPITAL + UP

Up.

ALT + CAPITAL + LEFT

Up un nivel.

ALT + CAPITAL + RIGHT

Download un nivel.

ALT + CAPITAL + ESPACIO

Insert indivisible narrow space.

ATL + F11

Basic.

ALT + F12

Options…

DRAW

FUNCTION KEYS

F1

Help.

F2

Text box.

F3

Group login.

F4

Position and size.

F5

Browser.

F6

Scrolling through the program bars.

F7

Spelling.

F8

Edit points.

F10

Activate the menu bar.

F11

Styles.

OTHER KEYS

SUPR

Delete content.

CAPITAL KEYS

CAPITAL + F3

Duplicate.

CAPITAL + F7

Automatic spell check.

CAPITAL + F10

Display the context menu.

CAPITAL + INSERT

Paste.

CAPITAL + SUPR

Cut.

CONTROL KEYS

CTRL +1

Line spacing 1.

CTRL + 2

Line spacing 2.

CTRL + 5

Line spacing 1,5.

CTRL + A

Open...

CTRL + B

Search.

CTRL + C

Copy.

CTRL + E

Select all.

CTRL + F

Search.

CTRL + G

Save.

CTRL + H

Search and replace.

CTRL + I

Cursive.

CTRL + J

Justified alignment.

CTRL + K

Cursive.

CTRL + L

Alignment to the left.

CTRL + M

Clean.

CTRL + N

Black.

CTRL + O

Open.

CTRL + P

Print.

CTRL + Q

Exit.

CTRL + R

Alignment to the right.

CTRL + S

Underlined.

CTRL + T

Centered alignment.

CTRL + U

New.

CTRL + V

Paste.

CTRL + W

Close window .

CTRL + X

Cut.

CTRL + Y

Redo.

CTRL + Z

Undo.

CTRL + [

Decrease.

CTRL +]

Increase.

CONTROL KEYS + FUNCTION KEYS

CTRL + F3

Leave group.

CTRL + F4

Close.

CTRL + F5

Sidebar.

CTRL + F7

Synonyms.

CONTROL KEYS + OTHER KEYS

CTRL + INSERT

Copy.

CTRL + +

Bring forward.

CTRL + -

Send back.

CTRL + /

Optional invisible separation.

CONTROL KEYS + CAPITAL KEYS

CTRL + CAPITAL + B

Subindex.

CTRL + CAPITAL + G

Group.

CTRL + CAPITAL + K

Combine.

CTRL + CAPITAL + M

Editing mode.

CTRL + CAPITAL + N

Templates

CTRL + CAPITAL + O

Print preview.

CTRL + CAPITAL + P

Superscript.

CTRL + CAPITAL + Q

Stop macro execution.

CTRL + CAPITAL + R

Rules.

CTRL + CAPITAL + S

Save as…

CTRL + CAPITAL + V

Special gluing.

CTRL + CAPITAL + Y

Repeat.

CTRL + CAPITAL + Z

Redo.

CTRL + CAPITAL + F4

Data origins.

CTRL + CAPITAL + F8

Fit to frame.

CTRL + CAPITAL + F10

Display the context menu.

CTRL + CAPITAL + ESPACIO

Insert indivisible space.

CONTROL KEYS + ALT KEY

CTRL + ALT + B

Search and replace.

CTRL + ALT + C

Coment.

CTRL + ALT + E

Extension manager.

CTRL + ALT + K

Hyperlink...

CTRL + ALT + CAPITAL + 9

Activate / Desactivate ItemBrowser.

CTRL + ALT + CAPITAL + G

DesGroup.

CTRL + ALT + CAPITAL + K

Split.

CTRL + ALT + CAPITAL + P

Pixel mode.

ALT KEY

ALT

Activate the menu bar.

ALT + BACKSPACE KEY

Undo.

ALT + CAPITAL + ESPACIO

Insert indivisible narrow space.

ALT + X

Switch Unicode notation.

ATL + F11

Basic.

ALT + F12

Options…

MATH

FUNCTION KEYS

F1

Help.

F3

Next error.

F4

Next mark.

F6

Scrolling through the program bars.

F9

Update.

F10

Activate the menu bar.

OTHER KEYS

SUPR

Delete content.

CAPITAL KEYS + FUNCTION

CAPITAL + F3

Previous error.

CAPITAL + F4

Previous mark.

CONTROL KEYS

CTRL + A

Select all.

CTRL + C

Copy.

CTRL + G

Save.

CTRL + N

New.

CTRL + O

Open.

CTRL + P

Print.

CTRL + Q

Exit.

CTRL + S

Save.

CTRL + U

New.

CTRL + V

Paste.

CTRL + W

Close window .

CTRL + X

Cut.

CTRL + Y

Redo.

CTRL + Z

Undo.

CONTROL KEYS + FUNCTION KEYS

CTRL + F4

Close.

CONTROL KEYS + OTHER KEYS

CTRL + INSERT

Copy.

CONTROL KEYS + CAPITAL KEYS

CTRL + CAPITAL + J

Full screen.

CTRL + CAPITAL + N

Templates

CTRL + CAPITAL + S

Save as...

CTRL + CAPITAL + F4

Data origins.

ALT KEY

ALT

Activate the menu bar.

ALT + X

Switch Unicode notation.

ATL + F11

Basic.

ALT + F12

Options…

ALT + BACKSPACE KEY

Undo.

BASE

FUNCTION KEYS

F1
Help.

F2
Formula. (Form)

F4
Preview. (Consultations)

F5
Execute consultations. (Consultations)

Browser. (Form)

F6
Scrolling through the program bars.

F7
Add tab or Consultation (Consultation)

Spelling. (Form)

F9
Update fields. (Form)

F10
Moving between the menu bar and the database menus.

F11

Styles. (Form)

F12

Numbered list. (Form)

OTHER KEYS

SUPR

Delete content. (Report)

ESC

Cancel.

INSERT

Insertion mode.

CAPITAL KEYS

CAPITAL + F3

Change capitalization. (Form)

CAPITAL + F7

Automatic spell check. (Form)

CAPITAL + F11

New style from selection. (Form)

CAPITAL + F12

Bulleted lists. (Form)

CAPITAL + INSERT

Paste. (Form / Report)

CAPITAL + SUPR

Cut. (Form / Report)

CONTROL KEYS

CTRL + A

Open... (Form / Report / Tables / Consultations)

CTRL + B

Search. (Form)

CTRL + C

Copy. (Form / Report / Tables / Consultations)

CTRL + D

Double underline. (Form)

CTRL + E

Select all. (Form / Report)

CTRL + F

Search registration. (Tables / Consultations)

CTRL + G

Save current registration. (Form / Report / Tables / Consultations)

CTRL + H

Search and replace. (Form)

CTRL + I

Cursive. (Form)

CTRL + J

Justified alignment. (Form)

CTRL + K

Cursive. (Form)

CTRL + L

Alignment to the left. (Form)

CTRL + N

New.

Black. (Form)

CTRL + O

Open. (Form)

CTRL + P

Print. (Form)

CTRL + Q

Exit. (Form / Report / Tables / Consultations)

CTRL + R

Alignment to the right. (Form)

CTRL + S

Underlined. (Form)

CTRL + T

Centered alignment. (Form)

CTRL + V

Paste. (Form / Report / Tables / Consultations)

CTRL + W

Close window . (Form / Report / Tables / Consultations)

CTRL + X

Cut. (Form / Report / Tables / Consultations)

CTRL + Y

Redo. (Form / Report / Tables / Consultations)

CTRL + Z

Undo. (Tables / Report)

CTRL + 0

Body text. (Form)

CTRL +1

Title 1. (Form)

CTRL + 2

Title 2. (Form)

CTRL + 3

Title 3. (Form)

CONTROL KEYS + FUNCTION KEYS

CTRL + F2

More fields... (Form)

CTRL + F3

Automatic text. (Form)

CTRL + F4

Close.

CTRL + F7

Synonyms. (Form)

CTRL + F8

Mark fields. (Form)

CTRL + F9

Field names. (Form)

CTRL + F10

Formatting marks. (Form)

CTRL + F12

Table. (Form)

CONTROL KEYS + OTHER KEYS

CTRL + INSERT

Copy. (Form)

CTRL + +

Calculate. (Form)

CTRL + -

Insert discretionary hyphen. (Form)

CTRL + /

Optional invisible separation. (Form)

CONTROL KEYS + CAPITAL KEY

CTRL + CAPITAL + B

Subindex. (Form)

CTRL + CAPITAL + I

Select text. (Form)

CTRL + CAPITAL + J

Full screen. (Form)

CTRL + CAPITAL + M

Editing mode. (Form / Report / Consultations)

CTRL + CAPITAL + N

Templates

CTRL + CAPITAL + O

Print preview. (Form / Report)

CTRL + CAPITAL + P

Superscript. (Form)

CTRL + CAPITAL + S

Save as... (Form / Report / Tables / Consultations)

CTRL + CAPITAL + V

Special gluing. (Form)

CTRL + CAPITAL + Y

Repeat. (Form)

CTRL + CAPITAL + Z

Redo. (Form)

CONTROL KEYS + CAPITAL + FUNCTION

CTRL + CAPITAL + F4

Data origins. (Form)

CTRL + CAPITAL + F8

Block area. (Form)

CTRL + CAPITAL + F11

Update. (Form)

CTRL + CAPITAL + ESPACIO

Insert indivisible space. (Form)

CTRL + CAPITAL + -

Insert indivisible hyphen. (Form)

ALT KEY

ALT + F11

Basic. (Form)

ALT + F12

Options. (Form / Report / Tables / Consultations)

ALT + BACKSPACE KEY

Undo. (Form)

CONTROL KEYS + ALT

CTRL + ALT + B

Search and replace. (Form)

CTRL + ALT + C

Insert Coment. (Form)

CTRL + ALT + E

Extension manager. (Form / Report / Tables / Consultations)

CTRL + ALT + K

Insert hyperlink. (Form)

CTRL + ALT + BELOW

Download a level in a list. (Form)

CTRL + ALT + UP

Up a level in a list. (Form)

www.ingramcontent.com/pod-product-compliance
Lightning Source LLC
Chambersburg PA
CBHW070450220526
45466CB00004B/1791